BEAUTIFUL Bible Verses

HARVEST HOUSE PUBLISHERS
EUGENE, OREGON

BEAUTIFUL BIBLE VERSES
Published by Harvest House Publishers
Eugene, Oregon 97402
www.harvesthousepublishers.com

Featuring selections from *100 Illustrated Bible Verses* by Workman Publishing Company, Inc., © 2015. Published under license.

ISBN 978-0-7369-6800-3

Printed in China

15 16 17 18 19 20 21 22 23 / LP-JH / 10 9 8 7 6 5 4 3 2 1

IN THE BEGINNING, GOD CREATED THE

Heavens

AND THE

Earth

GENESIS 1:1

& thou shalt Love the Lord thy GOD with ALL thine heart & with ALL thy Soul & with ALL thy might

DEUTERONOMY 6:5

4 Hear, O Israel: The LORD our God is one LORD:

5 And thou shalt love the LORD thy God with all thine heart, and with all thy soul, and with all thy might.

6 And these words, which I command thee this day, shall be in thine heart.

7 And thou shalt teach them diligently unto thy children, and shalt talk of them when thou sittest in thine house, and when thou walkest by the way, and when thou liest down, and when thou risest up.

King James Version

I CHRONICLES 16:31–34

31 Let the heavens be glad, and let the earth rejoice,
   and let them say among the nations, "The Lord is king!"

32 Let the sea roar, and all that fills it;
   let the field exult, and everything in it.

33 Then shall the trees of the forest sing for joy
   before the Lord, for he comes to judge the earth.

34 O **give thanks to the Lord, for he is good;**
   for his steadfast love endures forever.

New Revised Standard Version

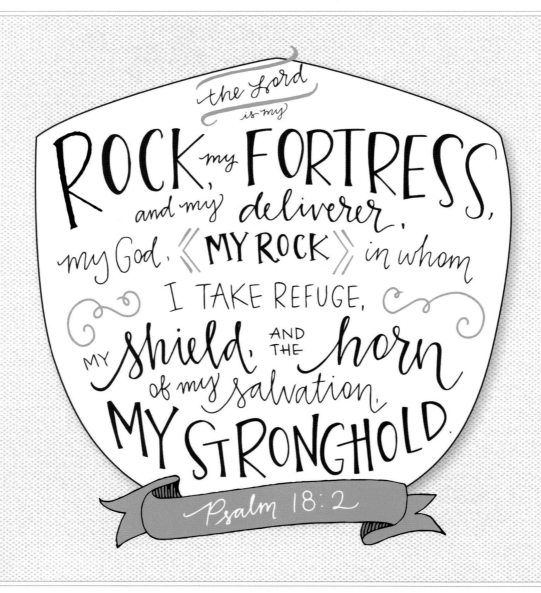

the Lord is my ROCK, my FORTRESS, and my deliverer, my God, ⟪MY ROCK⟫ in whom I TAKE REFUGE, my shield, and the horn of my salvation, MY STRONGHOLD.

Psalm 18:2

PSALM 18:1–3

1 I love you, O LORD, my strength.

2 The LORD is my rock, my fortress, and my deliverer,
my God, my rock in whom I take refuge,
my shield, and the horn of my salvation, my
stronghold.

3 I call upon the LORD, who is worthy to be praised,
so I shall be saved from my enemies.

New Revised Standard Version

FOR THOU ART
with me;
THY ROD & THY STAFF
they
COMFORT ME

PSALM 23:4 KJV

1 Come, let us sing to the Lord!

Let us shout joyfully to the Rock of our salvation.

2 Let us come to him with thanksgiving.

Let us sing psalms of praise to him.

3 For the Lord is a great God,

a great King above all gods.

4 He holds in his hands the depths of the earth

and the mightiest mountains.

5 The sea belongs to him, for he made it.

His hands formed the dry land, too.

6 Come, let us worship and bow down.

Let us kneel before the Lord our maker,

7 for he is our God.

We are the people he watches over,

the flock under his care.

New Living Translation

Take
firm hold o
instruction.
Don't let her go.
Keep her, for she is
your life.
–Proverbs
4:13

PROVERBS 4:10–15

10 Listen, my son, and receive my sayings.

The years of your life will be many.

11 I have taught you in the way of wisdom.

I have led you in straight paths.

12 When you go, your steps will not be hampered.

When you run, you will not stumble.

13 Take firm hold of instruction.

Don't let her go.

Keep her, for she is your life.

14 Don't enter into the path of the wicked.

Don't walk in the way of evil men.

15 Avoid it, and don't pass by it.

Turn from it, and pass on.

World English Bible

PROVERBS 30:2–6

2 "Surely I am the most ignorant man,
and don't have a man's understanding.

3 I have not learned wisdom,
neither do I have the knowledge of the Holy One.

4 Who has ascended up into heaven, and descended?
Who has gathered the wind in his fists?
Who has bound the waters in his garment?
Who has established all the ends of the earth?
What is his name, and what is his son's name,
if you know?

5 Every word of God is flawless.
He is a shield to those who take refuge in him.

6 Don't you add to his words,
lest he reprove you, and you be found a liar."

World English Bible

Every WORD of GOD is FLAWLESS. HE is a SHIELD TO THOSE WHO TAKE REFUGE in HIM.

PROVERBS 30:5

THE GRASS WITHERS

BUT THE OF GOD FORE

I S A I A

THE FLOWER
FADES

WORD

STANDS

V E R

H   40:8   WEB

JEREMIAH 29:10–12

10 This is what the Lord says: "When seventy years are completed for Babylon, I will come to you and fulfill my good promise to bring you back to this place.

11 For I know the plans I have for you," declares the Lord, "plans to prosper you and not to harm you, plans to give you hope and a future.

12 Then you will call on me and come and pray to me, and I will listen to you."

New International Version

For I know the Plans I have for you declares the Lord Plans to Prosper You and not to harm You Plans to give you Hope and a future

Jeremiah 29:11

You will SEEK ME & FIND ME WHEN YOU SEARCH FOR ME WITH ALL YOUR HEART.

JEREMIAH 29:13

13 You will seek Me and find Me when you search for Me with all your heart.

14 "I will be found by you," declares the Lord, "and I will restore your fortunes and will gather you from all the nations and from all the places where I have driven you," declares the Lord, "and I will bring you back to the place from where I sent you into exile."

New American Standard Bible

JEREMIAH 33:1–3

1 Then the word of the LORD came to Jeremiah the second time, while he was still confined in the court of the guard, saying,

2 "Thus says the LORD who made the earth, the LORD who formed it to establish it, the LORD is His name,

3 'Call to Me and I will answer you, and I will tell you great and mighty things, which you do not know.'"

New American Standard Bible

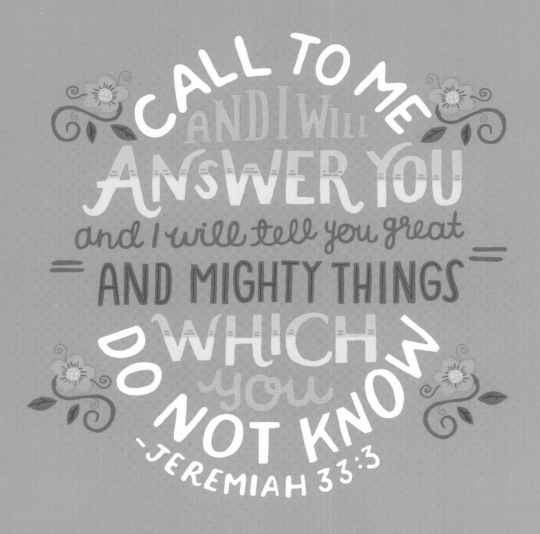

CALL TO ME AND I WILL ANSWER YOU and I will tell you great AND MIGHTY THINGS WHICH you DO NOT KNOW -JEREMIAH 33:3

LET YOUR LIGHT SHINE BEFORE OTHERS

MATTHEW 5:16

MATTHEW 5:13–16

13 "You are the salt of the earth; but if salt has lost its taste, how can its saltiness be restored? It is no longer good for anything, but is thrown out and trampled under foot.

14 You are the light of the world. A city built on a hill cannot be hid.

15 No one after lighting a lamp puts it under the bushel basket, but on the lampstand, and it gives light to all in the house.

16 In the same way, **let your light shine before others**, so that they may see your good works and give glory to your Father in heaven."

New Revised Standard Version

19 "Don't lay up treasures for yourselves on the earth, where moth and rust consume, and where thieves break through and steal;

20 but lay up for yourselves treasures in heaven, where neither moth nor rust consume, and where thieves don't break through and steal;

21 for where your treasure is, there your heart will be also."

World English Bible

Don't worry about tomorrow for tomorrow will bring its own worries

=MATTHEW 6:34=

31 "So don't worry about these things, saying, 'What will we eat? What will we drink? What will we wear?'

32 These things dominate the thoughts of unbelievers, but your heavenly Father already knows all your needs.

33 Seek the Kingdom of God above all else, and live righteously, and he will give you everything you need.

34 So **don't worry about tomorrow, for tomorrow will bring its own worries.** Today's trouble is enough for today."

New Living Translation

WHAT IS THE PRICE of TWO SPARROWS— ONE COPPER COIN?

MATTHEW 10:29 NLT

18 Jesus rebuked him, the demon went out of him, and the boy was cured from that hour.

19 Then the disciples came to Jesus privately, and said, "Why weren't we able to cast it out?"

20 He said to them, "Because of your unbelief. For most certainly I tell you, **if you have faith as a grain of mustard seed, you will tell this mountain, 'Move from here to there,' and it will move; and nothing will be impossible for you.**

21 But this kind doesn't go out except by prayer and fasting."

World English Bible

IF YOU HAVE FAITH
AS A GRAIN OF
MUSTARD SEED,
YOU WILL TELL THIS
MOUNTAIN,
'MOVE FROM HERE
TO THERE,' AND
IT WILL MOVE;

AND
NOTHING
WILL BE IMPOSSIBLE
FOR YOU.
MATTHEW 17:20

23 Jesus said to his disciples, "Most certainly I say
to you, a rich man will enter into the Kingdom of Heaven
with difficulty.

24 Again I tell you, it is easier for a camel to go
through a needle's eye, than for a rich man to
enter into God's Kingdom."

25 When the disciples heard it, they were exceedingly
astonished, saying, "Who then can be saved?"

26 Looking at them, Jesus said, **"With men this is
impossible, but with God all things are possible."**

World English Bible

"'LOVE THE LORD YOUR GOD WITH ALL YOUR HEART AND WITH ALL YOUR SOUL AND WITH ALL YOUR MIND.' THIS IS THE FIRST AND GREATEST COMMANDMENT.

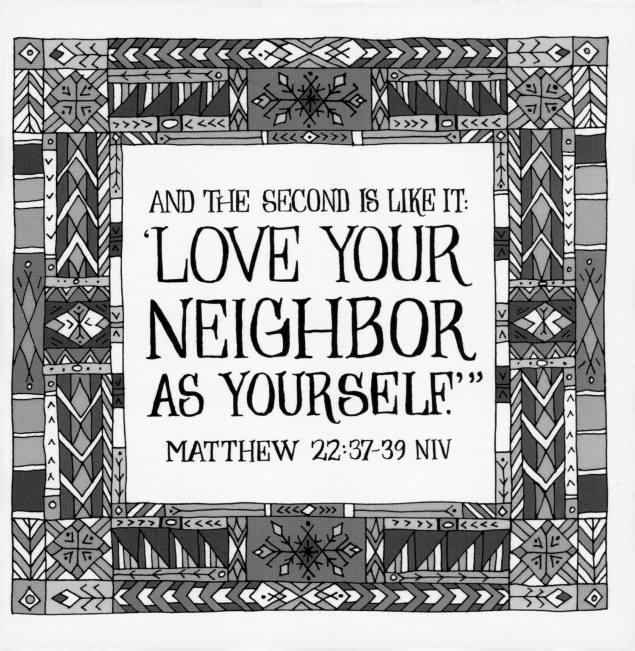

16 For God so loved the world that He gave His only begotten Son, that whoever believes in Him should not perish but have everlasting life.

17 For God did not send His Son into the world to condemn the world, but that the world through Him might be saved.

18 He who believes in Him is not condemned; but he who does not believe is condemned already, because he has not believed in the name of the only begotten Son of God.

19 And this is the condemnation, that the light has come into the world, and men loved darkness rather than light, because their deeds were evil.

20 For everyone practicing evil hates the light and does not come to the light, lest his deeds should be exposed.

21 But he who does the truth comes to the light, that his deeds may be clearly seen, that they have been done in God.

New King James Version

For God so **LOVED** the WORLD that He gave His Only begotten SON, that whoever BELIEVES in HIM should not perish -but have- EVERLASTING LIFE.

JOHN 3:16

Jesus said to them, I AM THE BREAD OF Life. He who comes to me shall never hunger, and he who believes in me shall never Thirst.

JOHN 6:35

32 Then Jesus said to them, "Most assuredly, I say to you, Moses did not give you the bread from heaven, but My Father gives you the true bread from heaven.

33 For the bread of God is He who comes down from heaven and gives life to the world."

34 Then they said to Him, "Lord, give us this bread always."

35 And **Jesus said to them, "I am the bread of life. He who comes to Me shall never hunger, and he who believes in Me shall never thirst.**

36 But I said to you that you have seen Me and yet do not believe.

37 All that the Father gives Me will come to Me, and the one who comes to Me I will by no means cast out.

38 For I have come down from heaven, not to do My own will, but the will of Him who sent Me.

39 This is the will of the Father who sent Me, that of all He has given Me I should lose nothing, but should raise it up at the last day.

40 And this is the will of Him who sent Me, that everyone who sees the Son and believes in Him may have everlasting life; and I will raise him up at the last day."

New King James Version

24 Martha said to Him, "I know that he will rise again in the resurrection at the last day."

25 Jesus said to her, **"I am the resurrection and the life. He who believes in Me, though he may die, he shall live.**

26 And whoever lives and believes in Me shall never die. Do you believe this?"

27 She said to Him, "Yes, Lord, I believe that You are the Christ, the Son of God, who is to come into the world."

New King James Version

I am the RESURRECTION & THE LIFE. HE WHO Believes in ME, though he may die, HE SHALL LIVE.

JOHN 11:25

Let not your heart be troubled, neither let it be afraid.

John 14:27 NKJV

31 "Do you now believe?" Jesus replied.

32 "A time is coming and in fact has come when you will be scattered, each to your own home. You will leave me all alone. Yet I am not alone, for my Father is with me.

33 I have told you these things, so that in me you may have peace. **In this world you will have trouble. But take heart! I have overcome the world."**

New International Version

IN THIS WORLD YOU WILL HAVE TROUBLE. BUT TAKE HEART! I HAVE OVERCOME THE WORLD.

-JOHN 16:33

ROMANS 12:1–2

1 I appeal to you therefore, brothers and sisters, by the mercies of God, to present your bodies as a living sacrifice, holy and acceptable to God, which is your spiritual worship. **2 Do not be conformed to this world, but be transformed by the renewing of your minds,** so that you may discern what is the will of God— what is good and acceptable and perfect.

New Revised Standard Version

I Corinthians 13:1–8

1 If I speak in the tongues of mortals and of angels, but do not have love, I am a noisy gong or a clanging cymbal.

2 And if I have prophetic powers, and understand all mysteries and all knowledge, and if I have all faith, so as to remove mountains, but do not have love, I am nothing.

3 If I give away all my possessions, and if I hand over my body so that I may boast, but do not have love, I gain nothing.

4 Love is patient; love is kind; love is not envious or boastful or arrogant

5 or rude. It does not insist on its own way; it is not irritable or resentful;

6 it does not rejoice in wrongdoing, but rejoices in the truth.

7 It bears all things, believes all things, hopes all things, endures all things.

8 Love never ends. But as for prophecies, they will come to an end; as for tongues, they will cease; as for knowledge, it will come to an end.

New Revised Standard Version

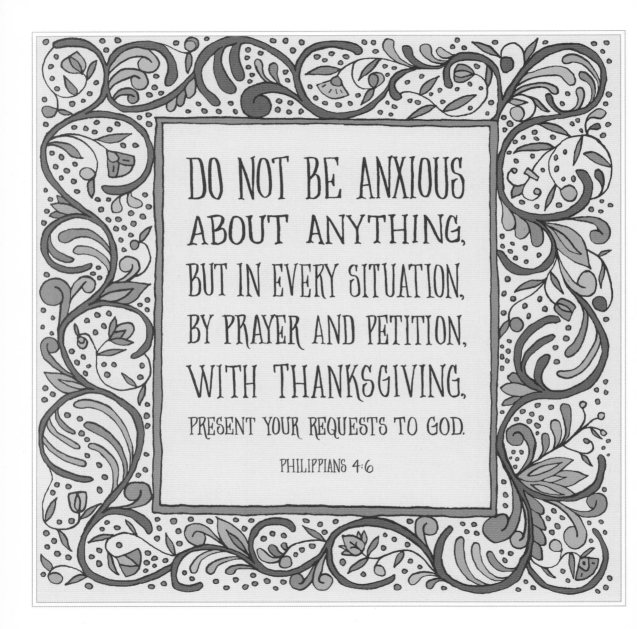

4 Rejoice in the Lord always. I will say it again: Rejoice!

5 Let your gentleness be evident to all. The Lord is near.

6 Do not be anxious about anything, but in every situation, by prayer and petition, with thanksgiving, present your requests to God.

New International Version

12b Everywhere and in all things I have learned both to be full and to be hungry, both to abound and to suffer need.

13 I can do all things through Christ who strengthens me.

New King James Version

I can do all things through **CHRIST** who strengthens me

philippians 4:13

7 For God has not given us a spirit of fear and timidity, but of power, love, and self-discipline.
8 So never be ashamed to tell others about our Lord. And don't be ashamed of me, either, even though I'm in prison for him. With the strength God gives you, be ready to suffer with me for the sake of the Good News.
9 For God saved us and called us to live a holy life. He did this, not because we deserved it, but because that was his plan from before the beginning of time—to show us his grace through Christ Jesus.

New Living Translation

1 Now **faith is the assurance of things hoped for, the conviction of things not seen.**

2 For by it the men of old gained approval.

3 By faith we understand that the worlds were prepared by the word of God, so that what is seen was not made out of things which are visible.

New American Standard Bible

BEHOLD, I Stand AT THE ANYONE HEARS if A DOOR THEN the TO HIM, & WITH HIM, AND

DOOR AND KNOCK.
MY VOICE AND OPENS
I WILL come IN
I WILL DINE
HE with ME.
REVELATION 3:20 NKJV

The Artists